Whispers from a Wardrobe

Whispers
from a Wardrobe

RICHARD EDWARDS

Illustrated by John Lawrence

LUTTERWORTH PRESS

CAMBRIDGE

Lutterworth Press
7 All Saints' Passage
Cambridge CB2 3LS

British Library Cataloguing in Publication Data
Edwards, Richard
Whispers from a wardrobe.
I. Title II. Lawrence, John
821'.914   PZ8.3

ISBN 0-7188-2683-3

First published 1987 by Lutterworth Press

Typeset in Monophoto Ehrhardt by
Vision Typesetting, Manchester
Printed in Great Britain by
St Edmundsbury Press Ltd
Bury St Edmunds, Suffolk

Contents

Big Bert

Big Bert sat on a cushion,
"I'm much too fat," moaned he,
"Who else could be so miserable?"
The cushion answered: "Me!"

Happy Easter

It was just a few days before Easter
When in through the beautiful door
Of Maxwell's Exotique Emporium
Swept Lady Belinda Fox-Gore.

Sebastian Sleek, chief assistant,
Oozed across with a smirk and a smarm
And bowed low in a glitter of Brylcreem,
Saying: "May I assist you, Madaam?"

"Yes," said Lady Fox-Gore with a whinny
And a waft of her elegant hand,
"You may bring me a box of soft nails
And a saxophone made out of sand;

"And I want a glass wig for my nephew
And a case of your happiest cheese
And a bottle of fog from Vienna
And a dozen young Oxfordshire fleas;

"Oh, I nearly forgot, bring an igloo
And some edible towels and a gong
And a cardboard guitar and a post box
And a fork with a wobbly prong;

"And two ounces of bone-china rhubarb
And a tortoise for warming the bed
And a packet of knotted spaghetti
And some liquid for polishing bread;

"Have you horses? Young Charlie loves horses,
So I'll take twenty-three of the best
And a pair of wire socks and a molehill
And one half of a plasticine vest;

"And a chair with five legs and a milk float
And a puddle to hang on the wall
And that thing over there with a helmet
And a couple of cod – and that's all."

Mr Sleek slaved away with brown paper
Till at last he had everything wrapped,
Then he wished Lady Gore: "Happy Easter,"
"Do you mean it's not Christmas?" she snapped.

"And I thought it was deepest December,
What a silly Milady am I,
Now I won't need a thing; please excuse me
But my taxi is waiting. Goodbye."

So she left with a flounce and a flourish
And a swish of the beautiful door,
While, dissolved into tears, poor Sebastian
Seeped away through a crack in the floor.

The Rain

I don't care what you say
I like
the rain,
I like it chucked like nails
against my win-
dow pane.

I don't care what you say
I like
the soak
of drizzle when it drifts
about the hills
like smoke.

I don't care what you say
I like
the flood
that makes our road the Nile
and leaves our lawn
all mud.

I don't care what you say
I like
it, so,
with hat and coat and yel-
low wellies, here
I go

on holiday to find
that fam-
ous plain
in Spain. I don't care what
you say, my friend,
I like
the rain.

Sad Sidney

Sad Sidney buttered a teacake
And buttered cream-crackers galore
And buttered his chair and the hearth-rug
And buttered across to the door.

Sad Sidney buttered the gatepost
And buttered the kerb of the street
And buttered along to the bus stop
And buttered upstairs to a seat.

Sad Sidney buttered the depot
And buttered his way out of sight
And buttered the road down to Portsmouth
And buttered the Isle of Wight.

Sad Sidney buttered the beaches
And buttered right up to the tide,
Then, finding his butter dish empty,
Sat down on the pebbles and cried.

The Man Outside

There's a man in the street
And I don't like his stare
And I don't like the look
Of his prickly hair
And I don't like his size
Or his shape, he's too thin,
And I don't like his slouch
Or his lopsided grin,
But I'm not at all scared –
Do you want to know why?
It's November the fifth
And his name is Guy.

The Statue

A statue of a lady wearing
Nothing but a frown
Had stood for centuries on a hill
Which overlooked the town
Until, fed up with standing still,
She suddenly climbed down.

The people in the ice-cream parlour
Blinked and rubbed their eyes
As in she walked and down she sat
To order "Peach Surprise."
The waiter wondered: could she be
A film star in disguise?

She ate and left so graciously
She wasn't asked to pay,
Then through the outskirts of the town
She made her marble way
Towards the shimmering meadows where
The wide blue river lay.

She rested on the riverbank
To bathe her stony toes,
And watched one ripple chase the next
As tiny fishes rose,
And giggled when a dragonfly
Tried landing on her nose.

At last, as shadows gathered round,
She walked the weary mile
Back up the hill to take her place
And dream of peaches while
The moon beamed on a statue wearing
Nothing but a smile.

Why?

Why are mirrors back to front?
Why aren't lemons sweet?
Why don't slugs have shells like snails?
Why don't snakes have feet?
Why does B come after A?
Why are ants so small?
Why don't carrots grow on trees?
Why is Malcolm tall?
Why won't rainbows come indoors?
Why won't custard fry?
Why do bats hang upside-down?
Why don't onions cry?
Why's tomorrow not today?
Why do heads have hair?
Why's a nettle not a rose?
Why aren't circles square?
Why don't horses moo like cows?
Why's July not May?
Why are your fingers in your ears?
Why are you running away . . . . .?

Whispers from a Wardrobe

A whisper from the wardrobe:
"It really isn't fair
To have to hang around here
With my arms up in the air."

A whisper from the wardrobe:
"It used to be a lark,
But now I'm tired of swinging
Like a monkey in the dark."

A whisper from the wardrobe:
"And where's my jacket gone?
It isn't very funny
To be left with nothing on."

A whisper from the wardrobe,
A sob, a tiny wail:
"Who'd be an empty coat-hanger
Upon an empty rail?"

Two of the Best

Some people have lisps,
Some people have sniffs,
Some people have snuffles and wheezes,
But no-one has anything quite to compare
With Uncle Fazackerly's sneezes:

They boom, they knock the bookshelves flat,
Whisk every whisker off the cat,
Start storms at sea and sudden squalls,
Make cracks, like spiders, run down walls,
Reduce the thickest rugs to rags,
Stream curtains out like battle flags,
Raise roofs, fuse lamps or smash a vase,
Stop dead the wheels of passing cars.
The last one blew poor Grandad's shirt
Clean off his back, while Grandma's skirt
Zipped out the door and next was seen
On someone's fence in Palmers Green,
And once, I heard a farmer say,
A sneeze blew all his sheep away.
Here's Uncle now. Let's ask . . . . . oh, no!
His nose is twitching . . . . . get down low!

ATCHOOO!

No, don't stand up; keep under cover;
They come in couples. Here's the other!

AAAAAATCHOOOOOOOOOO!!!

Some people have lisps,
Some people have sniffs,
Some people have snuffles and wheezes,
But no-one has anything quite to compare
With Uncle Fazackerly's sneezes.

Baa

Two very, very short-sheared sheep were standing on
    a hill,
One warmly mumbling to itself, one baa-ing loud
    with chill;
The cold one said: "I'm fro-o-o-o-zen stiff. How do
    you get your heating?"
The other answered with a smile: "That's easy:
    central bleating."

Round and Round

Rosie paints some dark green hills
Under a sky-blue sky,
Rosie paints a red-faced sun,
Some white doves flying high,
Rosie paints a man of straw
Beside the yellow wheat,
Rosie paints some coal black crows
That pick around his feet,
Rosie paints a big, grey cloud,
The cloud begins to rain,
The rain makes all her colours run,
Rosie starts again . . . . .

All the Bellvips

Where have all the bellvips gone?
Tell me, Lipperdoon.
Where is Bee the Bambleman?
Where's the lost malloon?
All across the nupper path
Sneeps an undud toon.
Where have all the bellvips gone?
Oh, tell me, Lipperdoon.

Tell me why Delinda's out,
Why, old Feem of Dee,
Dundledookies can't put ix
Where ix ought to be.
Lorps and linders snoof about
All as tusped as me.
Tell me why Delinda's out,
Oh, tell me, Feem of Dee.

Listen. On each pambled place,
On each hap and hoon
Tiny tinkas drip their noots
For the lost malloon;
I and Pie and old Ching-Chi
Must have sumpling soon.
Where have all the bellvips gone?
Oh, tell me, Lipperdoon.

Wait. A wipple in the wesp.
Look! It's Bamble Bee,
There's Delinda, there's the ix,
Bellvips, one, two, three!
Even the unlost malloon
Comes to cumble me.
Now I love you more than lunx!
Oh, thank you, Feem of Dee!

Saturday Night

I've tried counting frogs,
I've tried counting dogs,
I've tried counting millions of sheep,
I've counted my toes,
But I can't even doze,
Oh, how can I get to sleep?

My bed's full of bumps,
My pillow's all lumps,
My eiderdown's bunched in a heap,
I've heard a cat yowl
And the screech of an owl,
Oh, how can I get to sleep?

I've thought of a star
Where weary things are,
Like dream-hogs and snorpions that creep,
I've sucked on my thumb
So hard it's gone numb,
Oh, how can I get to sleep?

I've said all the rhymes
I know fifty times,
I'm fed up with Little Bo Peep,
Who cares that Miss Muffet
Sat down on a tuffet?
Oh, how can I get to sleep?

Now what's all that noise:
Chiming bells, yelling boys,
Passing traffic and sparrows going "cheep"?
It's quarter to ten,
Sunday morning again!
Oh, how did I get to sleep?

The Swan

Said the swan to its gliding reflection:
"May I ask you one question, my pet?
With a manner as stately and gracious as yours,
Tell me, why are your kisses so wet?"

The Secret Drawer

"Inside this wardrobe 'ere," says Des,
"There be one secret drawer
With treasures in, all tucked away
Behind one secret door.
To find that door," says Des, "you turns
One knob thing to the side,
To find that knob you got to shift
One hidden, secret slide,
To find that slide you got to raise
One secret, wooden flap,
To find that flap," says Des, "you reads
Instructions off a map.
And that's what's got me foxed," says Des,
"And what I'm frettin' for:
I've gone and left that map inside
The blinkin' secret drawer!"

Up Inside the Attic

Climb the shaking ladder,
Slide the rusty catch,
Brush away the cobwebs,
Wriggle through the hatch,
Balance on the rafters –
Inches from the sky –
Up inside the attic
Where the old things lie.

Here's a creaking suitcase
Crammed with secret things:
Lacy gloves and corsets,
Jars of curtain rings,
Collars, puppets, marbles,
Picture hooks as well,
Glittering Christmas tinsel
And a small brass bell.

Over in the shadows
Worn-out teddy bears
Lost in dreams of picnics
Snooze on broken chairs;
Shining high above them
Something seems to glow –
Just the dusty moonface
Of an old banjo.

What's this thing with handles?
What's that thing with feet?
Who left fourteen bed-springs
Underneath this sheet?
Look! A box of comics.
Look! A crate of toys.
What was that? Sh! Listen!
Something made a noise!

Quick! Across the rafters,
Wriggle through the hatch,
Down the shaking ladder,
Don't forget the catch,
Was there someone up there?
Probably just a mouse,
Couldn't be a nasty
In this nice old house.

There's the hall clock chiming:
Time for bed. Goodnight.
See you in the morning,
Happy dreams, sleep tight.
We'll go back tomorrow
Bravely, you and I,
Up inside the attic
Where the old things lie.

Rabbits, John and Jim

Two rabbits in a patch of sun
Were counting daisies one by one,
Jim made the total ninety-three,
"Oh, no," said John, "I can't agree;
I think you'll find it's ninety-two,
You've counted one twice, haven't you?"
"All right," said Jim, "I'll try once more."
This time it came to ninety-four.
"No, wrong again," said rabbit John,
"Why don't you put your glasses on?"
"I don't wear glasses," Jim said, "see?
Let's count together. One – two – three . . ."
This time John got to ninety-four,
But Jim said: "Ninety-five, I'm sure."
So off again went John and Jim,
While stars grew bright and day grew dim.

Now from the hedgerows can be heard
The tiny snores of beast and bird:
Mice, weasels, robins, sparrows, voles,
All fast asleep in nests and holes.
So who's that out there on the hill . . .?
Yes, John and Jim; they're counting still.

The Major

The Major inspected his garden
With a frown and a scowl on his face,
"You're a shambles," he barked, "all you flowers and
  things,
Where's your discipline? You're a disgrace.

"You roses should stand to attention,
And should brush all that mud off your roots,
And you hedges are due for a short back and sides,
I'll soon trim back those spiky green shoots.

"I'll shear you," he said to the bushes,
"I'll shave you," he said to the lawn,
"Tomorrow," he yelled at the trembling green,
"You will wish that you'd never been born!"

With that he strode off to the toolshed
To check that his gleaming array
Of clippers and mowers and bright secateurs
Would be ready for action next day.

He went to bed early that evening,
But as he lay trying to doze
The sudden, swift swish of a sharp piece of steel
Whistled down past the end of his nose.

And there, leaning over the bedside,
With a glittering, jagged toothed grin,
Stood the Scissorman waving his arms in the gloom
Like a nightmare that's forced its way in.

His body was two blades of metal
Crossing over and joined by a screw,
His face was the disc from a circular saw
And he said: "I've been looking for you."

Then he raised his sharp arm and the Major
Jerked awake in a terrified sweat –
For of course it *was* only a nightmare, but one
That the Major would never forget.

And very first thing the next morning
The Major marched down to his shed,
Which he padlocked with all of his cutters inside:
"And I hope you go rusty," he said.

So now it's a quite different Major
Who strolls round his garden for hours,
Surrounded by jungles of creepers and weeds
And roses with great floppy flowers,

And daisies and dahlias and damsons
And thickets of tall tangled trees
And brambles and birdsong and briony and buds
And butterfly bushes and bees.

Guess Me

Dear Reader,
   Guess me, I'm a riddle,
What's now my end
     was once my middle.
I don't wear fur
    or hair or wings,
My body's dressed
     in shiny rings.
I love the heap,
    I love the dark,
With twisting towers
     I leave my mark,
And move my pointed,
     questing nose
Not to, but underneath
    the rose.
Now ask me what
    I like to eat:
Old leaves and things,
     I won't touch meat,
And neither,
    if I had my wish,
Would Mr Mole
    or Mrs Fish.
Fantastic tunnels,
     close and curled,
Allow me through
     the underworld,
I wriggle, turn
    and sometimes squirm,
Yes, now you've guessed,
    Your best friend,

Some Favourite Words

Mugwump, chubby, dunk and whoa,
Swizzle, doom and snoop,
Flummox, lilt and afterglow,
Gruff, bamboozle, whoop
And nincompoop.

Wallow, jungle, lumber, sigh,
Ooze and zodiac,
Innuendo, lullabye,
Ramp and mope and quack
And paddywhack.

Moony, undone, lush and bole,
Inkling, tusk, guffaw,
Waspish, croon and cubbyhole,
Fern, fawn, dumbledor
And many more . . . .

Worm.

Sunlight or Surprise?

No, don't go near him, people say,
He's full of fleas, so keep away
From Old Jack Rags.

He's never tidy, never clean,
The filthiest tramp you've ever seen,
Is Old Jack Rags.

He lives on rubbish, sleeps in dirt,
He's only got one grubby shirt,
Has Old Jack Rags.

His teeth are black, his eyes are red,
He eats small children with his bread,
Does Old Jack Rags.

No, don't go near him, people say,
But I went near, just yesterday,
To Old Jack Rags.

And: "Do you sleep in dirt?" I said,
"And eat small children with your bread?
Well, Old Jack Rags?"

Then was it sunlight or surprise
That made those tears start from the eyes
Of Old Jack Rags?

A Cold Snack

A polar bear, fed up with fish,
Decided to eat flowers,
And searched across the snowy wastes
For hours and hours and hours,

Until at last he found a snow-drop
Growing through the ice,
A pretty flower but, thought the bear,
Just right for lunch, just nice.

He curled his paw to snatch it up,
Then stopped . . . Was that a squeak?
And nosing close he saw the snow-drop
Nod and start to speak:

"Oh, Mr Bear, I know I'm small
And you are like a hill,
But if you take one bite of me
I'm sure to make you ill,

"Your fur will turn all greeny-grey,
Loud clangs will fill your head,
And when you try to walk your feet
Will feel like lumps of lead.

"You won't know north from east or west,
You won't know left from right,
And awful dreams of kangaroos
Will wake you up at night."

The bear stepped back and rubbed a paw
Across his worried face,
Then grunted, turned and loped away
To find his fishing place;

While all around the blizzard wailed
And cruel winds loudly blew,
So no-one in the whole, white world
Could hear the snow-drop's: "Phew!"

Being So Small

Ashamed of being so small,
Ashamed of his lowly station,
Ashamed of having no clothes to wear,
No elegant conversation,
Ashamed of knowing no French,
Ashamed of being thought slimy,
Ashamed of having no horse to ride
And living where things were grimy,
Ashamed of looking so green,
Ashamed of not being a prince,
The frog jumped into a slithery ditch
And hasn't been heard of since.

Café Conversation

"Oo-er! A nasty maggot thing!"
Shrieked poor short-sighted Mabel,
But I shook my head and I answered "No
It's a bread-crumb on the table."

"Look!" Mabel gulped, "That woman's got
A squirrel on her head!"
But I shook my head, "A squirrel indeed!
It's a furry hat," I said.

"Be careful! There's a cobra on
That chair back!" Mabel cried.
But I shook my head, "It isn't a snake,
It's my school scarf," I replied.

Then Mabel's eyes gazed into mine
And this is what I heard:
"I think you're the handsomest boy in the room."
I didn't say a word.

The Beast and I

It has whiskers, fur and feathers,
And a tail and paws and wings,
Past the bracken stems it flickers,
Through the tops of trees it swings;
It's as fleeting as a shadow
And it hardly makes a sound –
Just a kind of rustling whimper
As it crosses open ground.

It's a slinking beast,
It's a jinking beast,
It's a dodge and lurk and scurry, it's a creeping
beast,
It's a won't show beast,
It's a tip-toe beast,
It's a scrabble on the gravel when you're sleeping
beast.

I remember waking early
On a white December dawn
To look out and see it standing
Like a statue on the lawn.
It was staring at my window
With a face so pale and thin,
And a look so cold and hungry
That I almost asked it in;
But our poodle started barking
And the beast got such a fright
That it turned and leapt the sundial,
Disappearing out of sight.

Now I won't rest till I've found it,
It's the beast I can't forget,
And I often go out searching
But I haven't found it yet;
One day soon we'll meet though, quietly,
In a place of calm and shade,
And I'll walk towards it smiling,
Saying "Please, don't be afraid."

It's a small, shy beast,
It's a sneak-by beast,
With no friends or close relations, it's an only beast,
It's an unnamed beast,
It's an untamed beast,
But I know at heart it's just a lost and lonely beast.

Lily

Lily's always dancing,
Through fields, down the lane,
In shops, her school, the cinema,
Out in the pouring rain.

Lily's always dancing,
Doing pirouettes and hops,
Mazurkas, mambos, arabesques,
Oh, Lily never stops.

Lily's always dancing,
With shadows, with the cat,
She saw a rainbow yesterday
And said: "I'll dance up that."

Lily's always dancing,
So up those steps of light
She skipped from indigo to green
To red to out-of-sight.

Lily's always dancing,
But why go quite so high?
I had to fetch my telescope
To search the darkening sky.

The last time I saw Lily
She was dancing past the moon,
I miss her more than anything –
Please, come back, Lily, soon.

The Marvellous Trousers

Last week on my way to a friend's birthday tea
I found them draped over the branch of a tree,
Oh, the Marvellous Trousers.

One leg was striped silver, the other striped blue;
I put them on, closed my eyes, wished and then flew!
Oh, the Marvellous Trousers.

They carried me up like a rocket, so fast
I ruffled the tail of each pigeon I passed,
Oh, the Marvellous Trousers.

I soared over Sicily, rolled over Rome,
And circled the Eiffel Tower on my way home,
Oh, the Marvellous Trousers.

I landed with ribbons of cloud in my hair,
But when I looked down at my legs – they were
    bare!
Oh, no Marvellous Trousers.

I know it sounds funny, I know it sounds weird,
But somehow and somewhere they'd just disappeared,
Oh, the Marvellous Trousers.

And when I explained at my friend's birthday tea,
The guests shook their heads and blew raspberries at
    me,
Oh, the Marvellous Trousers.

But I don't care tuppence: I've rolled over Rome,
I've circled the Eiffel Tower on my way home,
I've worn the Marvellous Trousers,
The Marvellous, Marvellous Trousers!

Nittle and Bubberlink

Quick was the Bubberlink, speedy was she,
Lived all alone in the fork of a tree,
Charged through the undergrowth, hurtled and leapt,
Raced through the forest while other things slept.

Slow was the Nittle and plodding and round,
Lived all alone in a hole in the ground,
Sauntered through barley fields, strolled in the corn,
Dawdled and dithered from dusk until dawn.

Sad was the Bubberlink, cheerless was she,
Sad was the Nittle, as glum as could be;
Each friendless evening they'd rise from their beds
Weeping a little and shaking their heads;

Till one warm night in the middle of June
As they roamed out by the light of the moon,
Suddenly crossing the same mothy space –
Nittle and Bubberlink came face to face.

Now, not too quickly, but neither too slow,
Down the dark lanes of the woodland they go:
Nittle and Bubberlink, hand in hand, friends,
Walking together until the world ends.

Just My Luck

"If weasels could fly," said my Grannie,
"I would give you four buckets of sweets,
Three mouse traps, two spoons and a tom-tom,
And lots more magnificent treats."

"Then give me them now, quick!" I shouted
As a furry thing whizzed past my throat,
But she shook her head answering "Sorry,
I said weasels, dear, that was a stoat."

Hide and Seek

Looking for Daisy
This way and that,
Try in the hayloft:
"Miaow," says the cat.

Looking for Daisy,
Haven't a clue,
Try in the farmyard:
The cow says, "Moo."

Looking for Daisy
All round the house,
Try in the cellar:
"Squeak," says the mouse.

Looking for Daisy,
Quite out of puff,
Try in the kennel:
The dogs says, "Ruff."

Looking for Daisy,
Oh, help me, please!
Try in the garden:
"Buzz," say the bees.

Looking for Daisy
Most of the day,
Try in the stable:
The horse says: "Neigh."

Looking for Daisy,
Where did she go?
Sitting and thinking:
Suddenly, "Bo!"

"Daisy! Oh, Daisy!
I must have walked miles.
Where were you hiding?"
Daisy just smiles.

The Wizard Said:

"You find a sheltered spot that faces south . . ."
  "And then?"
"You sniff and put two fingers in your mouth . . ."
  "And then?"
"You close your eyes and roll your eye-balls round . . ."
  "And then?"
"You lift your left foot slowly off the ground . . ."
  "And then?"
"You make your palm into a kind of cup . . ."
  "And then?"
"You *very quickly* raise your right foot up . . ."
  "And then?"
"You fall over."

Who?

I'm sure it wasn't me who spoke
When I was shinning up the oak,
So who, as I climbed up that tree,
Said: "Get those nasty feet off me!"

The Man of Many Brushes

He didn't leave his number,
We never knew his name,
But Wednesday afternoon at three
Was when the brush man came.

With white and bristly whiskers
That curled about his face,
He'd stand there on the polished step
And raise his tattered case:

"I have a brush for cupboards,
A brush for cleaning loos,
A brush to sweep your garden path,
A brush for sooty flues,

"A brush that goes round corners,
A brush for wicker chairs,
A brush for smelly dustbin lids,
A brush for plums and pears,

"A brush for tickling fancies,
A brush for tickling feet,
A brush for Auntie Agatha,
A brush for Uncle Pete,

"A brush for under beehives,
A brush for chocolate bars
That get so very sticky when
They fall off seats in cars,

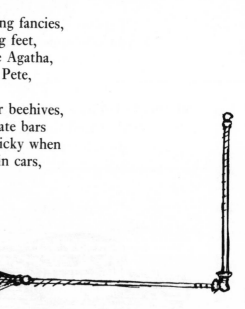

"A brush for brushing budgies,
A brush for puppy dogs,
A brush for finding little mice
That hide in piles of logs,

"And one rare brush of silver,
So soft and kind and light,
It brushes all your cares away
And glitters in the night."

And when he'd finished speaking,
He'd flick the polished clasp
That made his case fly open wide –
And made us gaze and gasp . . .

Of course, he doesn't come now,
And even for a mop
Or some old, silly scrubbing brush
We have to find a shop.

But I'll always remember
The man who came at three,
And when I'm feeling miserable
I shut my eyes and see

That one rare brush of silver,
So soft, so kind, so light,
It brushes all my cares away
And glitters in the night.

Surrey Dreams

I want to wear a stripey suit,
I want my voice to growl,
I want to click my claws, I want
To howl;

I want some whiskers round my nose
To test the forest breeze,
For fun I want to chase baboons
Up trees;

I want to steal in silence through
The alleys of the night,
I want to freeze, to spring, to fall,
To bite;

I want to track the hunter down
And when I crunch his gun,
I want to see his pink legs turn
And run;

I want to sleep on heaps of bones,
Safe in my jungle lair,
And when I wake I want my eyes
To glare;

I want to ambush buffalos
While spider monkeys scream . . .
But where do you find buffaloes
In Cheam?

Whistling

You put your lips together and you puff them out a bit,
You make a little circle and you blow some air through it.
My awful cousin Cathy says it's easier than pie:
If drippy weeds like her can do it, *why can't I?*

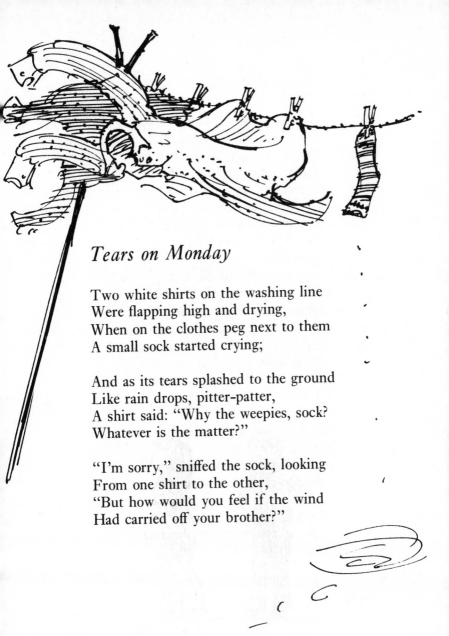

Tears on Monday

Two white shirts on the washing line
Were flapping high and drying,
When on the clothes peg next to them
A small sock started crying;

And as its tears splashed to the ground
Like rain drops, pitter-patter,
A shirt said: "Why the weepies, sock?
Whatever is the matter?"

"I'm sorry," sniffed the sock, looking
From one shirt to the other,
"But how would you feel if the wind
Had carried off your brother?"

A Confession

I've never seen a knuckerchuff,
I've never seen a yink,
I've never seen the tantwitch
With its fast and friendly blink,
I've never seen a wypish
Or a round mulungo boo,
I've never even seen a pair
Of clatts. Have you?

I've never heard the trumpet bird,
I've never heard the sound
Of napplebatters bleating
With their dops the wrong way round,
I've never heard the slash-shrimp
As it squoggles through the waves
With both its findips pointing
To the Karcapp Caves.

I've never travelled further than
A hundred zepps or so,
Or felt the urge to find the place
Where red gybeetums grow,
I've never raced a roondvoot,
Or played games of dandledark,
Or touched the magic feather
Of a loopo lark.

I've never been to Gungapland,
Or climbed the vast Tamdad,
I've never eaten smook or prump
Or nilp – I wish I had,
I've never watched a mooklet
Wriggle up *or down* a tree;
So what's this poem all about?
Well, don't ask me.

The Boastful Ghost

The boastful ghost flapped through a wall,
His white face full of glee,
"I'm much the bravest ghost there is,
A real ghoul," said he,
"All living creatures great and small
Are terrified of me."

Just then a bustling, bright-eyed mouse
Came hopping down the stair,
The ghost looked round, shrieked: "Help!" and flew
To tremble on a chair,
And, passing by, the tiny mouse
Was heard to squeak: "Oh yeah?"

Said Uncle

"There are people," said Uncle,
"Who bumble like bees.
There are people," said Uncle,
"With back to front knees.
There are people," said Uncle,
"Who breathe through one ear."
"There are people," said Auntie,
"Who shouldn't drink beer."

Bedtime

The night comes down on foxes
As they run across the hill,
The night comes down on fallow deer
That wander where they will,

The night comes down on white owls
As they wake in hollow trees,
The night comes down on badgers, free
To snuffle where they please,

The night comes down like velvet
On this house, and tenderly,
With starry streams and endless dreams
The night comes down on me.